FISHING: TIPS & TECHNIQUES ™

DEEP-SEA FISHING

CHRISTINE POOLOS

rosen publishing's
rosen central®

New York

Published in 2014 by The Rosen Publishing Group, Inc.
29 East 21st Street, New York, NY 10010

First Edition

Library of Congress Cataloging-in-Publication Data

Poolos, Christine.
Deep-sea fishing/Christine Poolos.—1st ed.—New York: Rosen, © 2014
       p. cm.—(Fishing : tips and techniques)
Includes bibliographical references and index.
ISBN: 978-1-4488-9486-4 (Library Binding)
ISBN: 978-1-4488-9502-1 (Paperback)
ISBN: 978-1-4488-9503-8 (6-pack)
1. Saltwater fishing. 2. Saltwater fishing—Juvenile literature. 3. Big game fishing.
4. Bait fishing. I. Title.
SH457.5 .P665 2014
799.16

Manufactured in the United States of America

CPSIA Compliance Information: Batch #S13YA: For further information, contact Rosen Publishing, New York, New York, at 1-800-237-9932.

CONTENTS

INTRODUCTION 4

CHAPTER 1 8
GETTING STARTED

CHAPTER 2 16
EQUIPMENT

CHAPTER 3 26
FINDING AND CATCHING FISH

CHAPTER 4 38
DANGERS AND SAFETY

CHAPTER 5 44
DEEP-SEA FISHING AND THE
ENVIRONMENT

GLOSSARY 52

FOR MORE INFORMATION 54

FOR FURTHER READING 58

BIBLIOGRAPHY 60

INDEX 62

INTRODUCTION

*I*magine you are on vacation with your family. Bored with trips to the beach and sightseeing, you convince your parents to take you fishing. You've seen fishermen and fisherwomen on the piers near your hotel with lots of lines in the water, hauling up catch every now and then. But you want to get out onto the open sea, on a boat, and see what happens.

You inquire at your hotel and are told to be at the marina early the next morning to make your reservation. You and your family arrive with some water, snacks, hats, and sunglasses, but no gear. You were told that rods and reels, bait, and everything else would be provided. The captain greets you right away and shows you around the boat. She takes special care to point out where the life vests are stowed and introduces you to her mate. You also meet some others who will be joining you on the trip.

Once you get out to sea, the captain turns off the motor and lets the boat drift. The sun is strong, the breeze light, and the smell of the sea unmistakable. The captain and her mate have been rigging the gear in preparation for this moment. They place

You might be lucky enough to reel in a swordfish like this one if you try your hand at deep-sea fishing.

the rods in outriggers along the sides of the boat and drop the lines straight down. Then you wait, enjoying the scenery and the experience. You see schools of fish under the surface and a few big ones leaping out of the water, but so far nothing is biting.

Suddenly one of the lines pulls and everyone jumps to their feet. It is your pole! The captain shows you how to hold the pole against your abdomen and work the reel. It's not as easy as just cranking the reel in; it's a give-and-take that requires a lot of patience. Soon, it also requires strength. At one point, you think you see your fish just below the surface. You can't see what it is, but it looks big and a little scary. Just as soon as it appears, it is gone, diving straight down and almost pulling you over the side of the boat.

The captain helps you let out the slack, then reels in a little. And then she decides it is time for the fighting chair. She sits you in a chair that is bolted to the deck but that pivots around from side to side and straps you in. Then she places the end of your fishing rod into the holder on the chair. From here on out, it's a struggle. The fish fights you, demanding every bit of strength you have. You're not sure how long it takes to reel in, but it feels like hours. Everyone on board is watching and yelling out tips and shouts of encouragement. The captain is right beside you, ready to take over if you get too tired. The mate has planted himself just next to your line. He is holding a long pole with a big hook at its end.

Just when the fish has begun to give up and lets you reel it in, the mate hooks the fish and brings it onboard through a little trap door on the side. Lots of seawater comes onboard with it. The fish is big, but not as huge as you'd imagined, and it is flopping around on deck. You let go of the pole, noticing that your hands are red and raw, and relax a minute. Then the mate asks if you want to watch him clean your fish—but not before your dad takes a photo of you next to your catch. While the captain helps out other passengers, the mate deftly guts and cleans your fish, then puts it on ice. You know you'll have a tasty dinner tonight.

Fishing is one of the great pastimes in the United States. There are many different kinds of fishing, including freshwater fishing, fly fishing, saltwater fishing, pier fishing, and even fishing with bow-and-arrow. All have their benefits, and how and where you fish is a personal preference.

Deep-sea fishing has several unique benefits. First, because you're off the coast, deeper into the sea, you have the opportunity to hook a greater variety of fish. The biggest and best fish swim off the coast in deeper waters. And because you're on a boat, not limited by land and the angle of your pole, you can drop your line straight down to the ocean floor. If that doesn't work, you can try different angles. If the fish aren't biting where you are, you can easily move to another location. And you can use technology to find them.

Deep-sea fishing is an exciting and potentially dangerous activity that is never dull. It can take a little extra planning, and it can cost you more money than other kinds of fishing. But few fishing trips will give you the adrenaline rush and the potential for reeling in a fish as big as your little brother.

CHAPTER 1

GETTING STARTED

*I*f you're not an experienced "angler" (another word for fisherman and fisherwoman), deep-sea fishing might seem intimidating at first. Perhaps you've never held a fishing pole in your life. Or maybe you've been working your local fishing hole for years but are afraid of what lurks in the sea. After all, there's quite a difference between a 1-pound (0.5 kilograms) crappie and a 55-pound (25 kg) grouper.

The first thing to remember is that, although deep-sea fishing is on an entirely different scale than most other types of fishing, it is above all a fun, oftentimes thrilling, pastime. That doesn't mean you won't need to learn new techniques and rules and that you don't need to take safety precautions. But the opportunity to broaden your fishing horizons is totally worth it.

What Is Deep-Sea Fishing?

Also known as offshore fishing, open-water fishing, sport

Deep-sea fishing is a thrilling and adventurous pastime. Working with an experienced crew member is essential for first-timers.

fishing, or, sometimes, big-game fishing, deep-sea fishing is the pursuit of fish in deep ocean water—nearly 100 feet (30 meters) or deeper—well off the coast. In deep ocean waters, the variety of catch is very different. Fish are larger and heavier, and it takes a lot more experience to catch them and haul them in. It also takes strong equipment and a lot of patience. You might be fighting a 100-lb (45 kg) fish for more than two hours!

Trying your hand at deep-sea fishing also requires knowledge of the sea. Experienced sea anglers learn about which ocean currents and tides yield the best catch. They also know what conditions to look for when searching for fish. It would be foolish to simply motor a boat out to sea, cast a line into the ocean, and hope for the best. There is a lot more to deep-sea fishing.

But don't be put off by all that you don't know. If you're not an experienced deep-sea angler, there are plenty of resources to get you started.

Finding a Boat

One of the first things to consider before you go deep-sea fishing is how you're going to get on the water. If you live near a coast and have your own boat—good for you! You can cross one thing off your list. If you venture out in your own boat, chances are you or someone joining you has all the knowledge you need to embark on such a journey. The ocean can be dangerous. You will need someone with knowledge of tides, currents, winds, and charts. He or she must also be adept at using radios and other communication equipment in case something goes wrong. And that doesn't even cover the experience needed to catch fish on the open seas.

But if you don't own your own sea boat, you're going to need to enlist some help. Fortunately, there are options. Your best bet is to seek an experienced captain who charters fishing trips. If you live near the coast, you can visit a local bait shop or pro shop and ask how to find such captains. The shop's employees and customers will steer you in the right direction. Or visit your local marina and talk to some captains and collect brochures. If you want to fish while you're on vacation, do some research on the Internet, or ask an employee at the hotel where you'll

Boat Dos and Don'ts

The following is a collection of tips from the Web site of Majesty Fishing, a deep-sea charter boat company in Atlantic Beach, Florida. It is typical of many charter companies' rules and recommendations:

This vessel is family oriented—NO Drunkenness or foul language. A 48-quart (45 liter) cooler is the maximum size to fit under the bench; all coolers must fit under the benches. Keep in mind it's only a day trip; most people want to pack like they are going on a 3-day fishing trip, so pack light. A cooler is not required for any reason; lunch and refreshments may be purchased onboard if you would like. We keep the fish in our boxes on ice all day, and the crew will clean the fish upon arrival back to the dock and put them in Ziploc baggies. The crewmembers do work for tips; around 15 percent is customary...You are welcome to bring your own tackle and/or rod and reels; at least 60 lb (27 kg) test is recommended. We fish with 80 lb (36 kg) test. A maximum of 3 rods per person...[B]ring along some sunscreen, a good attitude, and a beginner for their way with luck.

be staying. It is important to find a boat far in advance because many outfits require reservations and get booked up quickly.

Party Boats

One way to go is by booking a spot on what is informally known as a party boat. Party boats are large boats designed to hold a lot of people,

Party boats can get very crowded, so arrive early to get an optimal spot. They are a great, affordable option for a novice deep-sea angler.

from 60 to 140 anglers. Usually they operate on a first-come, first-served basis, so if a party boat does not require reservations, it is best to get in line early to nab a good location on the boat.

There are many advantages to fishing from party boats. First, it's relatively inexpensive. It can cost as little as $25 to $30. Second, party boats can be a great way to learn deep-sea fishing techniques. The captain and crew are very knowledgeable about fishing in those particular waters. They know where to go, where to move if the fish aren't biting, what the best bait is, and generally the best way to ensure fishing success.

If you don't have your own, chances are you can rent tackle on the party boat. The boat will also provide bait and chum. Perhaps better yet, the mates are there to assist you. They will set your hooks, offer advice, and, for a minimal fee, clean your fish for you.

For all their crowdedness, party boats do feature many comforts that can make a day of fishing more pleasant. These often include cushioned bench seating, restroom facilities, and snack bars where you can purchase food and drinks. They are also outfitted with the proper safety equipment, including life vests, flotation devices, GPS, first-aid kits, and radios.

Party boats are in the business of transporting a lot of people offshore in the interest of having a fun day catching lots of fish. Trips may be scheduled for a few hours or a whole day. Since the boat is packed with people, it is especially important to exhibit proper etiquette. You'll need to make sure you don't cross lines with anyone, and always be courteous to the other fishermen and fisherwomen. In addition, at the end of the trip, it is customary to tip the mates 10–15 percent of the cost of the trip if they have helped you.

Private Charter Boats

Another option for those who don't have access to a boat is to charter one. In this case, research is your friend. Because you will be essentially hiring a captain and his or her boat to take you on a private fishing trip, it is important to find out all you can about the outfit. If you can get recommendations from other anglers, so much the better, but it doesn't hurt to interview the captain yourself. Be prepared to ask as many questions as you want. You should find out about safety equipment onboard, the captain's licensing and level of experience, the fish species he or she targets, what you'll need to bring onboard, and the price per day. And don't forget to tell him or her about your level of experience and any special needs you or your party may have.

OFFSHORE FUN

This group has chartered a boat for two days of deep-sea fishing. On this chartered boat, they will get the privacy, amenities, and expert instruction they desire.

Generally, charter boats are smaller outfits with room for fewer people. If you have enough people in your party, you may have the boat to yourself. However, to keep costs down, captains often try to fill the boat to capacity, so they may book two or three smaller parties together in the name of cost effectiveness.

Speaking of money, one potential drawback to chartering a boat is cost. If money is no object, then it shouldn't be a concern. But as with any private endeavor, you'll pay more for exclusivity—in this case, personal access to an experienced captain. Chartering a boat usually depends on the size of the boat and the time spent on the sea. Depending on those factors, expect to pay several hundred or even a thousand dollars or more a day for a charter.

Since a charter boat is smaller than a party boat, expect to bring your own provisions, especially food and drink. You will be at one with the sea, with close access to the water, and amenities may be few to none. However, much of the trip is taken care of for you. The captain will most likely provide prepared bait. The crew will help you with everything from teaching techniques, rigging lines, and setting bait, to helping you fight and haul in your catch. Cleaning fish is also part of the fee. Most important, you will get close, individual attention from the captain and crew. If you don't mind being out at sea on a smaller boat, the abundance of information you can learn on a good charter boat is immeasurable.

CHAPTER 2

EQUIPMENT

Deep-sea fishing is an activity that requires some advance preparation. Even if you have experience yourself or will be accompanied by an experienced deep-sea angler, you need to be familiar and armed with the proper equipment. Put aside any visions you have of ambling down to your local creek with a pole, a line, and a hook to see if the fish are biting. Deep-sea fishing requires some serious gear. But remember to consider whether any of this equipment will be provided for you on the boat you'll be riding on.

Gear

The first thing you will need to prepare for your deep-sea fishing adventure is "tackle." This is a general term for your gear, meaning your rod, reel, lines, and hooks. Since you will be fighting against fish that may weigh between 30–100 pounds (14–45 kg), you will need a specialized saltwater rod and reel and heavyweight lines. If you are purchasing tackle, talk to a knowledgeable salesperson and specify the kind of fishing you'll be doing and the species you'll be pursuing. There are countless combinations of tackle, and you want to be sure to use one that will give you a competitive advantage over the fish.

Aside from the basics, you should bring your own lures and sinkers, unless the outfit provides them for you. Lures, bait, and sinkers are heavier for deep-sea fishing than for freshwater fishing. Different fish are attracted to different tackle, so it helps to know what species you'll be pursuing. The Internet is a valuable resource for learning all about successful lures for various species. Everyone's experience is different, but it never hurts to start with what's worked for others. If you are fishing with an experienced captain or guide, he or she will be able to offer you guidance or provide you with a well-chosen lure.

Keep your tackle in a waterproof tackle box or bag. Particularly if you are fishing from a party boat, you want to make sure you have all your gear at the ready. When that big fish comes, you won't have a lot of time to be searching the deck for your things. This also ensures that another angler doesn't mistake your gear for his or hers. Some other items to store in your tackle box are clippers for cutting line, forceps for removing hooks, and a knife to clean your fish. Again, party boats and charter boats most likely will provide at least some of these tools for you.

Before stepping on a boat, make sure you have brought your fishing license along. Depending on the regulations of the state in which you are fishing, even though the boat you're using needs to be licensed, each angler may also need to possess a license. Some charter boats sell licenses, so call in advance or check their Web site for information. You can also purchase a license at local bait shops, online, or in department stores with fishing sections, such as Wal-Mart. It is a good idea to store your license in a sealed plastic bag while onboard so that it can't be ruined by seawater or rain. In some states, charter boats have what is called a "charter license," which allows you to fish legally under their license.

Finally, you should bring something to keep your catch in once you've hauled it out of the ocean. A charter boat should provide coolers and ice for your catch, and party boats may have refrigerated holds. If your boat does not, you should bring your own cooler or garbage bag filled with ice to preserve your catch until you can clean it and cook it up for dinner.

Onboard

The equipment onboard will most likely be provided by the charter or party boat. However, it is a good idea to check the Web site of the outfit or call ahead to make sure the boat you'll be riding on comes equipped with all the necessary accessories.

First and foremost, the boat should contain enough life vests for every passenger. If you are bringing children along, make sure the boat can furnish child-size life vests, as they might not carry them onboard. Larger boats should carry lifeboats or flotation devices in the event that something happens to the boat and passengers need to evacuate. Before you set sail from the marina, the captain or crew should address these safety concerns and announce the onboard location of these emergency items. Mechanical failure or damage to the boat could mean that you need to abandon the ship.

Crews of party boats and charter boats are there to help. This mate prepares to clean and store a fish caught by a passenger.

The boat should also carry one or several first-aid kits. Whenever you put yourself into a situation involving hooks, knives, sharp teeth, and a slippery deck, the potential for accidents exists. Because of the intensity of off-shore fishing, someone is bound to at least cut a finger or hand. It is important to have sterilizer, antibiotic creams, bandages, pain relievers, and other items on hand for basic first-aid fixes.

The boat should come stocked with buckets for various needs. For instance, you will need to keep your bait and ballyhoo in a bucket of seawater to ensure its freshness. You may also want to hold your haul in a bucket of sea-water until you can clean it and put it on ice at the end of the trip.

Even if you bring your own rod and reel, you might need help hauling in a monster catch. Deep-sea anglers often turn to gaffs—long poles with a large, sharp hook at the end—used to

spear the fish for greater ease in bringing it onboard. Gaffs are especially useful when your fishing line isn't strong enough for the fish

A fighting chair is a valuable aid when reeling in a big, strong fish. It can provide leverage and a measure of comfort if the fish takes a long time to give up the fight.

you're reeling in. There is nothing worse than reeling in a big one, only to have your line snap before you can haul in the catch.

If you're going on a longer trip, you may need a reverse-osmosis water-maker, which converts saltwater to freshwater. If you are at sea for several days or weeks and cannot bring along enough bottled water, the water-maker can make ocean water drinkable.

Most boat captains and guides know that anglers can use all the help they can get. Therefore, it doesn't hurt to have a fishfinder on board. A fishfinder is a device that uses sound waves to locate schools of fish and structures like reefs or ship wreckage where fish may be feeding.

Commercial Fishing Equipment

Although they may be pursuing some of the same fish as recreational anglers, commercial fishers use entirely different equipment to haul in their catch. To snag a large supply of huge fish like tuna and swordfish, hooking them one at a time would be far too inefficient. These men and women are paid by the haul, so the goal is the capture of a large quantity of fish in a short amount of time. Depending on the species, commercial fishermen and fisherwomen set out traps or nets that they reel up using a pulley system. They may throw out trotlines rigged with dozens of hooks. They are more likely to use harpoons than the similar, smaller gaffs. Those fishing for clams, oysters, and scallops use a device called a dredge, which scrapes the ocean floor and collects the mollusks as the boat travels.

Depending on the size of your boat, it may feature several structures that make fishing easier and more pleasant. Most boats have rod holders that allow you to fit your rod in and leave it alone until something bites. Outriggers are poles that extend out into the water to which you attach your line, eliminating the chance of tangling your line with someone else's. Most exciting of all is the fighting chair, a pivoting chair that is secured to the deck and features a sort of seatbelt and a holder for your rod. When you have a bite and you determine that you've got a big fish that's ready for a fight, you need some leverage. Many anglers prefer to strap themselves into the fighting chair and leverage their rod while they fight the fish. For those who prefer to stand, your boat might include harnesses equipped with a gimbal—a rod holder—to provide the same kind of leverage.

What to Wear

Since you'll be on the boat all day, it is important to equip yourself with the right clothing and accessories. At sea, the elements are more intense than on land; and sun, wind, and cool temperatures can get in the way of a fun and successful fishing trip.

First, make sure you are dressed properly. The key is to dress in layers. If you're fishing at the height of summer or in a tropical location, you can probably get away with shorts or light pants and a T-shirt. But if the wind picks up, you'll be happy you brought a windbreaker or sweatshirt. In cooler climates, you'll want to add a few more layers, such as long underwear and a fleece jacket, and perhaps a hat and gloves. Remember, though, to wear light layers. This is because you might need to wear a life vest, and it can be uncomfortable trying to squeeze on a life vest over a bulky sweatshirt and jacket. Because the deck gets slippery from water and fish guts, wear shoes or boots with stable rubber bottoms. It's also wise to be prepared for inclement weather.

Wearing waterproof foul-weather gear keeps you dry and warm at sea.

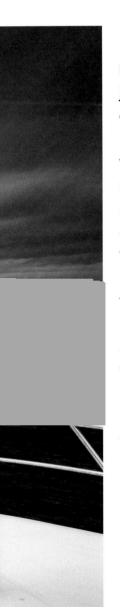

Pack foul-weather gear like a hooded poncho or waterproof jacket, as well as a change of clothes so that you can be dry on the way home, when temperatures have dropped.

When you're out on the ocean, the sun reflects off the water and can feel blinding. Bring a pair of good sunglasses, preferably polarized, and a hat with a brim. The hat can also protect your head and face from the sun. Consider bringing a hat with a chinstrap so that it doesn't blow off your head when the wind picks up. The sun can also burn your skin, so be sure to stay covered if possible, and wear sunblock with the highest SPF you can.

Even if it's a warm day, bring along a pair of gloves with a rubber grip tread on the palm side. These will provide useful traction when you're handling anything slippery and will protect your hands from cuts when pulling up a line, grappling with a spiny or razor-toothed fish, or cleaning your fish with a sharp knife.

CHAPTER 3

FINDING AND CATCHING FISH

Once you have packed your gear and prepared for your deep-sea fishing trip, it's time to focus on the fishing itself. If you have not fished before, or if you have only fished in freshwater or close to shore, it is essential that you enlist the help of an experienced angler. Whether it is a friend, family member, or a charter captain, guide, or crewmember, be open to asking for help and learning as much as you can about off-shore fishing techniques.

Factors to Consider

As enjoyable and exciting as offshore fishing may be, it's not simply a matter of throwing a line in the water and reeling in a trophy fish. At sea, there are many factors to consider, such as wind, current, tides, species, time of year, and even time of day. Even the most experienced

The best anglers know how to read the tides and currents to find fish, such as this sailfish.

offshore anglers are challenged by the mysteries of the sea. They know how to switch up their techniques and rigs for optimum success.

Tide and Current

You will find fish wherever they can find food, and fish food is affected by tide and current. Currents can trap bait and flotsam for fish to feed on. Tides also affect where fish hang out and how they feed. Generally, running tides—tides that are either rising or falling—are the best time to catch fish. Successful anglers know to adjust other factors if tide and current conditions are not optimal. Fast tides usually lead to better off-shore fishing conditions. This is because the visibility is better and the water is less choppy. If the tide is slower, it might be best to change up the fishing spot and move closer to rocks or wreckage. It may also be a good time to chum the water, since the chum will stay near the boat (more on chum later in this chapter). It is also advisable to change your targeted species, as some types of fish bite more on slow tides and others on fast tides. Captains and guides can consult tide charts prior to departure in order to plan the best time to search out fish.

Water Temperature

Fish cannot survive in water that is either too warm or too cold for them. The ocean temperature affects the water's clarity. Therefore, it is important to understand where the water temperature is ideal for fish. For deep-sea anglers, satellite images of sea temperatures are an invaluable resource.

Weather

Aside from the air and water temperature, the wind and barometric pressure are useful clues to help you find fish. If you are out on a day when there is bright sun, fish might delve down away from the surface into cooler waters. Cloud cover might bring them out because they feel safe. If the barometric pressure, or air pressure, rises or drops considerably, fish know that a storm may be moving in or out. They will know it is a good time to either feed or lay low.

Big-Game Fishing

Big-game fishing is a sport pursued around the world. The standard bearer for record keeping is the International Game Fish Association (IGFA). The IGFA keeps world records and focuses efforts on conservation and safe fishing practices.

Chances are your catch will not be a record holder. However, you should know the potential of what you might reel in. Following are some of the weights of the IGFA's current record holders.

- Blue marlin: 1,402 pounds (636 kg)
- Pacific halibut: 459 pounds (208 kg)
- Mako shark: 1,221 pounds (554 kg)
- Red snapper: 50 pounds (23 kg)
- Yellowfin tuna: 405 pounds (184 kg)
- Atlantic cod: 98 pounds (44 kg)
- Black grouper: 124 pounds (56 kg)

Location

In the United States, you can try your hand at offshore fishing almost anywhere along the East, West, or Gulf coasts. Since water temperatures, structures, and food sources vary, each region has its favorite catches. Before planning a trip, know the migratory patterns of your sought-after species to make sure they'll be in your area at that particular season. Alaska offers some of the country's largest halibut and salmon. Hawaii boasts perhaps the best variety of fish, and the activity can be enjoyed there all year long.

Species

Saltwater fish are generally bigger, faster, and stronger than freshwater fish. In addition, you will find a greater variety in the sea than in your local pond, lake, or river. The best fishermen and fisherwomen know what to pursue in their area, but they also know how to change tack and adjust to the pursuit of a different species depending on the conditions. Following are just a few of the larger categories of fish you might see if you are lucky enough to go deep-sea fishing.

- **Bluefish:** Bluefish are a great way to start. Bluefish can weigh 30 pounds (14 kg) and seem to want to bite anything, so they also provide a good opportunity for offshore novices. The fish is so named because it appears blue in the water.
- **Flatfish:** Flatfish is a category of fish that includes winter flounder (found in deep water in the summer), fluke (found in deep water in winter and spring), and halibut, which can weigh hundreds of pounds.
- **Cod, grouper, and tuna:** Cod like cold water and can weigh from 30 to 200 pounds (14 to 91 kg). Grouper stay toward the bottom. Tuna like deep water and will travel far. There are many varieties, and they can weigh up to 1,500 pounds (680 kg). They are very fast and will put up a fight.
- **Marlin:** The marlin is one of the offshore angler's most coveted prizes. There are several types of marlin, but the blue marlin can weigh 1,800 pounds (816 kg) and measure 16 feet (5 meters) long. This fish travels at incredible speeds and leaps out of the water to great heights. It's no wonder so many seek the challenge of catching a marlin!

Some fish present greater challenges than others and are therefore more coveted trophies. Others are great catches for beginners. Whatever you catch, make an effort to cook it up for dinner. There are few greater pleasures than getting to eat a fish you caught yourself.

Deep-Sea Fishing Techniques

The best, but most general, tip when it comes to deep-sea fishing is to learn the habits of the fish. Learn where the fish feed, what they feed on, and what water temperatures they prefer. Once you start to understand the fish, then you will know how and where to find them. But that is only half the battle. It is not enough to find a fish. You must also know how to lure and catch it.

Finding the Fish

There are several approaches to finding fish, depending on the factors discussed above. One of the simplest ways is to follow the birds. Birds will swoop down and feed on certain types of fish that might also be food for the fish you're pursuing. If you notice several birds flying in one direction, keep your eye on them. It might be worth heading in their direction and taking advantage of their feast.

One of the best methods for attracting fish is to chum. This method involves throwing a bag of ground-up bait over the side of the boat into the water. If you know a school of fish is nearby, this is a great way to get their attention. You can also use a method called "chunking." With this technique, you grind the chum even finer and throw it onto the water surface, creating a sort of slick. Then, when the fish start taking notice, throw small bait at them to get them to stay. These methods are good for fast-swimming fish that tend to take off if they don't find food right away, such as tuna.

A mate baits the lines on his boat in hopes of catching a white marlin. He has decided to use mackerel, ballyhoo, and mullet while trolling.

Another method is trolling. With this approach, the captain motors the boat at slower speeds with several lines in the water to see if anything bites. With trolling, anglers generally keep their rods in the gunwales, or pockets on the side of the boat, or on outriggers that keep the line perpendicular to the ocean surface.

Sometimes captains use sonar to locate an underwater structure such as a reef or wreckage. These structures are magnets for fish because they contain all kinds of plants and smaller fish for the larger fish to feed on. When a captain locates a concentration of fish, he or she may turn off the power, anchor the boat, and drop the lines straight to the ocean floor. This method is called bottom fishing.

Drifting is similar to bottom fishing, except that the boat's anchor is not dropped. The boat drifts with the tide and current. You can fish straight to the bottom or at mid-level depths when drifting, depending on the type of fish you wish to catch.

Luring the Fish

The best offshore anglers have definite opinions about what works for them when it comes to attracting fish, based partly on experience and luck and a little bit of superstition. The best thing to do is to get advice from a captain or crewmember or anyone

This fish fell for a very convincing lure and paid the price for it. Experienced anglers know the best combination of bait, lures, and sinkers to catch prize fish.

who has experience fishing the specific waters you're in.

In general, to lure a fish, you will want to offer it what it wants most in the world: food. The simplest way to do that is to attach half a shrimp or a small fish to your hook and cast it in the water. Sometimes this works and a fish will take the bait. Some fish, however, are smarter than that. They know better than to fall for that trick. In those cases, experienced anglers lure them in with a little something special.

Fishermen and fisherwomen use all kinds of configurations of bait and lures and sinkers to attract various species under various conditions. Again, all of the variations are too numerous to discuss here, but most rigs include a lure and some bait. The lure is a visual that may look like a fish, such as a piece of shiny metal or a skirt, which looks sort of like a tassel and keeps the bait from attracting foul things in the water. The bait is either natural or artificial fish.

One of the best types of bait for deep-sea fishing is ballyhoo, a small fish that anglers prepare ahead of time to help them catch fish. By popping the spine and rigging it on a line, the small fish appears to be dancing on the water as the boat trolls. The big fish are attracted to the ballyhoo, which they think is swimming on the ocean's surface, and move in for the bite.

This man takes advantage of a fighting chair to reel in his catch. Since the fish may not give up the fight right away and may be quite heavy and powerful, it helps to have a safe, comfortable, securely anchored seat from which to wage the battle.

Hauling In and Handling Your Catch

Once you feel a bite on your line, the fun begins. This is when you enlist help from anyone around you, which hopefully is someone with experience. The fish might be reeled right up, but with deep-sea fishing, you never know. You could be in for a struggle that takes minutes or even hours.

The important thing is not to panic. Have someone help you secure your pole for the leverage you'll need while fighting the fish. If you prefer to stand, have someone buckle a harness around your waist. If you are nervous about slipping on the deck, someone will strap you into the fighting chair.

Patience will be your friend. You will need to learn the give-and-take of the line—when to use your strength to reel in and when it's time to give the fish some slack. Chances are, others on the boat will be excited and happy to help as your adrenaline reaches new heights. After a struggle, as you reel the fish in, someone wearing gloves or using a gaff will help you haul the fish onboard.

If you are on a charter boat, one of the crew will most likely whisk away your fish and either put it in a bag on ice or clean it right away. Before that happens, make sure someone takes your picture next to the fish so that you never forget exactly what it looked like.

CHAPTER 4

DANGERS AND SAFETY

There's no doubt that those who participate in offshore fishing are attracted to its drama and excitement. The notion of being out on the high seas, fighting against a big tuna or marlin, and showing your friends a photograph of the one that didn't get away is very appealing. These are reasons why so many anglers enjoy the sport.

But there are dangers to think about as well. The sport just wouldn't be as exciting if there were no risk involved. Nevertheless, that doesn't mean you can't take precautions to minimize those risks. One of the greatest ways to ensure a successful and enjoyable fishing trip is to make sure you protect yourself from danger by focusing on safety.

On the Sea

Even before you pick up a pole, you must practice boat safety. When you first board the boat, pay attention to any opening

It is extremely important to listen carefully to and obey all instructions, orders, and safety precautions issued by your captain and crew. It's especially crucial to pay attention before the excursion begins and the distractions of fishing divert your focus.

remarks given by the captain and crew. Make sure you know where the life vests are stowed and how to get to them quickly if an emergency arises. Find out what to do in case of other emergencies like capsizing, damage to the boat, and rough weather. Your captain will have specific instructions for how to handle such emergencies.

Since you will be on the water for at least several hours, this is no time to realize you forgot to pack something essential. Not only will you be uncomfortable during your trip, but you might also be risking your health. Remember to bring with you water, food, sunscreen, and other sun protection (like a hat and sunglasses). Even if you've been on

The Importance of Onboard Sobriety

Even if your boat permits alcohol, members of your group should think twice before drinking. First of all, even people who think they can hold their liquor may be surprised at how they are affected by drinking onboard. The sun increases levels of inebriation and the chance of dehydration. An inebriated person will have difficulty navigating around a rocking boat, and the swells of the waves may cause seasickness. Inebriation in close quarters can lead to erratic behavior and perhaps even confrontations and scuffles, which can greatly detract from what should be an enjoyable day.

Second, the dangers inherent in fishing under the best conditions are magnified when alcohol enters the picture. Alcohol impairs judgment, reaction time, and coordination and increases the likelihood of accidents. A sliced hand or a hooked finger can be incredibly painful, especially when you're out at sea and can't receive proper medical care for hours. Severely inebriated anglers are in danger of slipping and hitting their heads on the side of the boat or other structures. They are also in greater danger of falling overboard.

Do yourself a favor and don't increase your risks of having an accident on your fishing trip. Deep-sea fishing is a pleasurable, high-intensity, dramatic sport on its own. Alcohol can only dim, dampen, and endanger the day's enormous potential for adventure and excitement.

a boat before and had no problems, it's not a bad idea to take some anti-seasickness medication about an hour before sailing. There is nothing worse than feeling a wave of nausea with every swell of the sea.

Finally, make sure you or your parents research the outfit you'll be using for your trip. Make sure the captain and his or her boat are properly licensed, have a clean operating and safety record, are outfitted with proper safety features, and have not exceeded passenger capacity.

Know the proper etiquette when fishing on a boat with others. Be respectful of the other anglers' space, and be sure not to get your lines crossed.

Precautions and Etiquette

Think about all the equipment you use to fish, and then consider how dangerous it can be if it's not used safely. For instance, much of the gear is sharp, slippery, or unwieldy. In close quarters, it's not unusual for an angler to hit fellow anglers with a pole or hook them while casting off. It's almost a rite of passage to hook your own finger while baiting and rigging.

Deep-sea fishing involves the use of many sharp and dangerous tools. Exercise caution when using knives and hooks, and protect your hands with a dry and grippy pair of gloves.

When your hands are already slimy, attempting to clean a slippery fish with a sharp knife can be especially dangerous. Take the time to either towel off your hands or slip on some gripping gloves. And speaking of slippery, exercise caution when walking around the deck. It can become quite slippery from water and fish guts. This danger is magnified when you're fighting a fish and need all the stability you can get.

After you've reeled in a massive fish, the last thing you'll be thinking about is safety. But be cautious during this time because a huge fish from the sea can present some dangers when flopping around on deck. Depending on the fish, it may have sharp teeth or other bony and cutting structures that could harm you or someone else. Make sure a crewmember is nearby and ready to take care of the fish right away.

CHAPTER 5

DEEP-SEA FISHING AND THE ENVIRONMENT

I t can be difficult to think about the environment when you're out on the sea wrestling a 50-pound (23-kg) halibut. But, in some ways, it is an ideal time to consider how we impact our planet's resources. Though you might think that one person can't make much of a difference, your time fishing the seas will give you an opportunity to witness an ecosystem up close.

As with hunting, think of fishing as a sport. Just as hunters value the land and the animals that live on it, anglers respect the sea and its inhabitants. If we all fished irresponsibly, eventually there would be nothing left in the sea to pursue. Therefore, it is important to educate yourself on matters related to conservation and responsible fishing practices.

Catch-and-Release

One of life's great pleasures is cooking up a few

This angler is practicing catch-and-release. After hauling up a marlin he has caught, he will photograph it for posterity and then throw it back into the ocean.

freshly caught fish for dinner. And there is nothing wrong with pursuing a big trophy fish, taking a picture of yourself standing next to it, and perhaps even mounting it on a wall. However, you might also consider taking a different approach by throwing back what you've caught. Catch-and-release can be a fun and gratifying way to spend a fishing trip. After all, the real challenge lies in pursuing, hooking, and reeling in the fish. After you've done that, send the fish back into the ocean to live a good life and reproduce, thereby guaranteeing future fish stocks.

When you release the fish back into its habitat, you first want to make sure the fish is unharmed. That means you might have to use special bait and hooks to ensure the fish goes back in the water fully intact. Your captain can help you select the proper hooks. If a hook is deeply embedded, it sometimes is best to simply cut the line and not harm the fish further by forcing out the hook. Usually the hook will work its way out on its own or decompose in the fish.

It is better if you do not handle the fish very much after catching them because fish have a protective coat of slime that is harmed when you touch them. Either keep the fish in water while you dehook it, or make sure your hands are wet in order to minimize removal of the slime. Try not to drop the fish on deck so that the fish does not suffer internal damage. Also, try not to touch or block the gills. This will impair the fish's breathing.

Particularly with offshore fishing, you may have struggled for a long period and exhausted the fish. It would be unfair to toss a tired fish back into the water. Revive the fish by placing it in a bucket of saltwater or by gently holding it in the current for several minutes. Then direct the fish toward the current so that it can ease back into the water.

Conservation

Because of commercial and, to a lesser extent, recreational fishing, some species are in danger of extinction. In addition, pollution and other human-generated stresses upon the ocean have impacted the entire ecosystem. If a species' food or feeding spot is taken away, it will die off. There are also natural reasons why a species might be endangered. For example, sharks are challenging and exciting to catch, but they reproduce very slowly. Therefore, overfishing does not give the population time to catch up and replenish its numbers.

Wildlife and Sport Fish Restoration Program

In 1950, Congress passed the Dingell-Johnson Sport Fish Restoration Act, which emulated 1937's Pittman-Robertson Wildlife Restoration Act. The legislation placed a tax on fishing equipment and tackle that would in turn fund conservation programs. The Wallop Breaux amendments to Dingell-Johnson, passed in 1984, extended such taxes to boat fuel and import duties.

Federal and state governments cooperate on sport fish restoration efforts. Funds from the Wildlife and Sport Fish Restoration Program go to the management of fisheries, protection of waters and coastal wetlands, creation of designated structures for boaters, and educational outreach efforts that teach the public about conservation.

The result of the program is that the fishing waters are cleaner and more productive, conservation efforts are researched and enforced, and new generations of anglers learn about the importance of fishing responsibly. To learn more about the Wildlife and Sport Fish Restoration Program, go to http://wsfrprograms. fws.gov/Subpages/AboutUs/AboutUs1.htm.

Fortunately, most states have developed guidelines and laws to aid preservation. Your captain or guide can educate you regarding local laws, particularly if you're a visitor to the area. Be sure to keep only as many fish as the law allows. Make sure the fish you keep meet the size requirements as stated by the law. In addition, your captain should make sure that he or she is as far from the coast as the law requires

Fishery biologists study the patterns of fish species and influence fishing laws. Their work helps ensure fish populations continue to grow and thrive.

when you begin to fish. Also, some states regulate the season in which certain species can be fished, just as there are seasons for hunting deer and other animals. In short, it is a good idea to be aware of the local laws. You will find them on the Web site of the state's wildlife and game commission, or you can ask your captain or guide.

What Is Being Done

Scientists who study and manage our world's fish population are called fishery biologists. These biologists study the patterns and conditions of various species and consider the needs of fisheries and fishermen and fisherwomen. They interview anglers about the number and size of fish they've caught. They also tag fish and record their growth and migration patterns over time. With this information in hand, fishery biologists devise plans for keeping species alive. If they discover that a species is being overfished, they will advise game and wildlife commissions to adjust limit, size, and season laws accordingly. This helps revive and restore a fish population and ensures that the species can continue to be fished far into the future.

This research and other efforts to improve the health of fisheries and fish populations are funded by the sale of licenses. They are also aided in part by the federal government. Reports from fishery biologists and lobbying by conservation groups are used to set and alter federal and state laws and guidelines.

What You Can Do

It is important to follow local laws and release your catch if possible. But there are other things you can do to help the environment when you're fishing. For instance, make an effort not to litter. You may think it's not a big deal to throw trash into the ocean. After all, it's a big body

This shark has become entangled in a plastic bag. The trash is encircling the shark's gills, compromising its air supply. It is important to avoid littering in the ocean while you are deep-sea fishing.

of water and the litter will probably just wash up on shore for someone else to throw away. Before that can happen, however, the trash can negatively affect the ecosystem by introducing an invasive species or harmful chemicals. In addition, you may throw something overboard that chokes a dolphin or fish.

If you find anything suspicious in the water or see suspicious behavior by others, report it to your captain or to the local authorities when you return to shore. It's up to all of us to make sure the laws are being followed. If you see someone breaking these laws, you are obligated to do something about it.

Get involved in conservation efforts. Even if you are visiting a fishing area on vacation, see what conservation programs are offered. A great way to spend one of your vacation days could be volunteering to assist them in their efforts, perhaps by helping clean a stretch of coastline or heading out on the ocean as a cleanup volunteer or research assistant. Also research your local conservation programs and join the organizations that sponsor them. Not only will you learn a lot about conservation and aquatic life and health, but, in the process, you may learn even more about fishing.

GLOSSARY

angler A fisherman or fisherwoman.

bait Real or artificial food used to attract fish.

ballyhoo A small fish that is particularly effective bait for ocean fish.

catch-and-release Throwing hooked fish back into the water.

charter boat A craft that can be rented for private or semiprivate use.

chum Chopped-up bait thrown into the water to attract fish.

chunking Throwing out chunks of fish to attract other fish.

current The horizontal movement of water.

dredge Device used to pull up mollusks and other organisms from the ocean floor.

drifting Trailing a line behind a boat that has cut its motor and drifts with the tide and current.

ecosystem Community of interacting living organisms and their environment.

fighting chair A chair secured to a boat's deck from which you can gain leverage to fight and reel in fish.

fishfinder A device that uses sonar to locate fish in deep water.

flotsam Wreckage in the sea, such as a shipwreck.

forceps Pincers or tweezers used to de-hook or pick bones from a fish.

gaff A long pole with a large, sharp hook at one end, used to haul fish onboard.

gunwale The sides of a boat, often furnished with pole holders.

harpoon Large spear used to catch whales and other large sea creatures.

lure An object attached to the end of a line that visually attracts a fish because it looks like something the fish would feed on.

mollusk Classification of invertebrates that includes snails and mussels.

novice An inexperienced person; someone who is new to an activity or pursuit.

outrigger A structure that projects off the side of the boat, allowing a fishing line to drop straight down, far off the side of the boat.

party boat A larger boat that holds more anglers.

polarized sunglasses Sunglasses that restrict harmful light rays and reduce sun glare on reflective surfaces like water or snow.

rig To prepare a line by tying on a hook, lure, bait, and sinker.

sinker A weighted object tied to a line that keeps the bait from floating on the surface of the water.

tackle A general term for fishing equipment.

tide The vertical movement of water, caused by gravitational forces of the sun and moon.

trolling Trailing a line behind a boat that is moving at slow motor speeds.

water-maker A device that uses the process of reverse-osmosis to convert seawater to water that is safe to drink.

Association of Fish and Wildlife Agencies
444 North Capitol Street NW, Suite 725
Washington, DC 20001
(202) 624-7890
Web site: http://www.fishwildlife.org
The Association of Fish and Wildlife Agencies represents North
America's fish and wildlife agencies to advance sound, science-
based management and conservation of fish and wildlife and their
habitats in the public interest.

Department of Fisheries and Oceans Canada
200 Kent Street
13th Floor, Station 13E228
Ottawa, ON K1A 0E6
Canada
(613) 993-0999
Web site: http://www.dfo-mpo.gc.ca
Fisheries and Oceans Canada (DFO) and its Special Operating Agency,
the Canadian Coast Guard, deliver programs and services that
support sustainable use and development of Canada's waterways
and aquatic resources.

Fisheries and Habitat Conservation Program
Department of the Interior
1849 C Street NW
Washington, DC 20240
(800) 344-WILD [9453]
Web site: http://www.fws.gov/FHC
The Fisheries and Habitat Conservation Program is unique within the
U.S. Fish & Wildlife Service in its abilities to apply a dual approach

to natural resource management: it focuses on both helping manage species and helping to conserve their habitats.

International Game Fish Association (IGFA)
300 Gulf Stream Way
Dania Beach, FL 33004
(954) 927-2628
Web site: http://www.igfa.org
The International Game Fish Association is a nonprofit organization committed to the conservation of game fish and the promotion of responsible, ethical angling practices through science, education, rulemaking, and recordkeeping.

Marine Conservation Institute
4010 Stone Way N, Suite 210
Seattle, WA 98103
(425) 274-1180
Web site: http://www.marine-conservation.org
The Marine Conservation Institute is a nonprofit organization dedicated to saving our living oceans. It works with scientists, politicians, government officials, and other organizations around the world to protect essential ocean places and the wild species in them.

National Coalition for Marine Conservation
4 Royal Street SE
Leesburg, VA 20175
Web site: http://www.savethefish.org
The National Coalition for Marine Conservation (NCMC) is the USA's oldest public advocacy group dedicated exclusively to conserving

ocean fish, such as swordfish, marlin, sharks, tuna, striped bass, menhaden, and herring.

National Oceanic and Atmospheric Administration (NOAA)
NOAA Fisheries Service
1315 East West Highway
Silver Spring, MD 20910
Web site: http://www.nmfs.noaa.gov
NOAA's National Marine Fisheries Service is the federal agency responsible for the stewardship of the nation's living marine resources and their habitat. Its National Marine Fisheries Service is responsible for the management, conservation, and protection of living marine resources within the United States' Exclusive Economic Zone, which is water between 3–200 miles (5–322 km) offshore.

U.S. Fish and Wildlife Service
Department of the Interior
1849 C Street NW
Washington, DC 20240
(800) 344-WILD [9453]
Web site: http://www.fws.gov
The mission of the U.S. Fish and Wildlife Service is working with others to conserve, protect, and enhance fish, wildlife, plants, and their habitats for the continuing benefit of the American people.

Wildlife and Sport Fish Restoration Program
Department of the Interior
1849 C Street NW
Washington, DC 20240
(800) 344-WILD [9453]

Web site: http://wsfrprograms.fws.gov/home.html
The U.S. Fish and Wildlife Service's Wildlife and Sport Fish Restoration (WSFR) Program works with states, insular areas, and the District of Columbia to conserve, protect, and enhance fish, wildlife, their habitats, and the hunting, sport fishing, and recreational boating opportunities they provide.

World Wildlife Fund
1250 24th Street NW
Washington, DC 20037
(202) 293 4800
Web site: http://wwf.panda.org/what_we_do/how_we_work/conservation /marine
WWF's Global Marine Programme creates, promotes, and implements solutions to protect marine ecosystems and use marine resources sustainably.

Web Sites

Due to the changing nature of Internet links, Rosen Publishing has developed an online list of Web sites related to the subject of this book. This site is updated regularly. Please use this link to access the list:

http://www.rosenlinks.com/FISH/Deep

FOR FURTHER READING

Bourne, Wade. *Basic Fishing: A Beginner's Guide*. New York, NY: Skyhorse Publishing, 2011.

Campbell, Dave. *Beginner's Guide to Fishing: and Survival Guide for Supervising Adults*. Seattle, WA: CreateSpace, 2010.

Carpenter, Tom. *Saltwater Fishing: Snapper, Mackerel, Bluefish, Tuna, and More*. Minneapolis, MN: Lerner, 2012.

Craven, Charlie. *Charlie's Fly Box: Signature Flies for Fresh and Salt Water*. Mechanicsburg, PA: Stackpole Books, 2010.

Diamond, Paul. *Fishing's Greatest Misadventures*. Birmingham, AL: Wilderness Press, 2008.

Evanoff, Vlad. *How to Fish in Salt Water*. Seattle, WA: CreateSpace, 2010.

Evanoff, Vlad. *Surf Fishing*. Seattle, WA: CreateSpace, 2010.

Greenlaw, Linda. *All Fishermen Are Liars: True Adventures at Sea*. New York, NY: Hyperion, 2005.

Greenlaw, Linda. *Seaworthy: A Swordboat Captain Returns to the Sea*. New York, NY: Penguin Books, 2011.

Hall, Jerold "Buck." *Sportsman's Best: Offshore Fishing*. Stuart, FL: Florida Sportsman, 2007.

Kamberg, Mary-Lane. *Salt Water Fishing* (Fishing: Tips and Techniques). New York, NY: Rosen Central, 2012.

Kaminsky, Peter, and Greg Schwipps. *Fishing for Dummies*. Hoboken, NJ: For Dummies, 2011.

Mozer, Mindy. *Pier Fishing* (Fishing: Tips and Techniques). New York, NY: Rosen Central, 2014.

Philpott, Lindsey. *Complete Book of Fishing Knots, Lines, and Leaders*. New York, NY: Skyhorse Publishing, 2008.

Pollizotto, Martin. *Saltwater Fishing Made Easy*. Camden, ME: International Marine/McGraw-Hill, 2006.

Rivkin, Mike. *Big: The 50 Greatest World Record Catches*. Seymour, CT: The Greenwich Workshop Press, 2008.

Rivkin, Mike. *Big-Game Fishing Headquarters: A History of the IGFA*. Dania Beach, FL: IGFA Press, 2006.

Thomas, William David. *Deep Sea Fishing*. New York, NY: Benchmark Books, 2010.

Underwood, Lamar. *The Greatest Fishing Stories Ever Told: Twenty-Eight Unforgettable Fishing Tales*. Guilford, CT: The Lyons Press, 2004.

White, Randy Wayne. *Randy Wayne White's Ultimate Tarpon Book: The Birth of Big Game Fishing*. Gainesville, FL: University Press of Florida, 2012.

BIBLIOGRAPHY

Bannerot, Scott, and Wendy Bannerot. *The Cruiser's Handbook of Fishing*. Camden, ME: International Marine/Ragged Mountain Press, 2003.

Cacutt, Len. *Big-Game Fishing Handbook*. Mechanicsburg, PA: Stackpole Books, 2000.

Editors of Creative Publishing. *Salt Water Fishing Tactics: Learn from the Experts at Salt Water Magazine*. Minneapolis, MN: Creative Publishing International, 1999.

International Game Fish Association. "Conservation for Ethical Sport and Productive Science." Retrieved August 2012 (http://www.igfa.org/Conserve/main.aspx).

Krebs, Dave. "Testimony Submitted to the Appropriations Committee Subcommittee on Commerce, Justice, Science and Related Agencies of the U.S. House of Representatives." Retrieved August 2012 (http://www.appropriations.house.gov/_files/gulfofmexicoreeffishshareholdersalliance.pdf).

Matson, Bradford. *Deep Sea Fishing: The Lure of Big Game Fish*. San Diego, CA: Thunder Bay Press, 1995.

OutdoorAlabama.com. "Sport Fish Restoration." Retrieved September 2012 (http://www.outdooralabama.com/research-mgmt/sport-fish.cfm).

The Outdoor Guy. "Beginner's Guide to Offshore Fishing." Retrieved August 2012 (http://www.theoutdoorsguy.com/2011/06/beginners-guide-to-offshore-fishing).

TakeMeFishing.org. "Catch and Release." Retrieved August 2012 (http://www.takemefishing.org/fishing/fishopedia/fishing-and-conservation/catch-and-release).

TakeMeFishing.org. "Finding Salt Water Fish." Retrieved September 2012 (http://www.takemefishing.org/fishing/saltwater-fishing/where-to-fish/factors-for-finding-saltwater-fish).

Toth, Mike. *Fishing Basics*. New York, NY: Penguin, 2000.

Unkart, John. *Offshore Pursuit*. Edgewater, MD: Geared Up, LLC, 2006.

Wildlife and Sport Fish Restoration Program. "Wildlife and Sport Fish Restoration Program." U.S. Fish and Wildlife Service. Retrieved August 2012 (http://wsfrprograms.fws.gov).

World Fishing Network. "Deep Sea Fishing." Retrieved August 2012 (http://www.worldfishingnetwork.com/fishing/deep-sea-fishing.aspx).

INDEX

B

ballyhoo, 20, 35
big-game fishing, 29
bluefish, 30
bottom fishing, 33

C

catch-and-release, 44–46
charter boats, 10, 13–15, 17, 18, 37
charter licenses, 18
chum/chumming, 13, 28, 31
chunking, 31
clothing, 23–25
cod, 29, 30
commercial fishing equipment, 22
conservation, 46–51

D

deep-sea fishing, explanation of, 8–10
drifting, 33

E

etiquette, 13

F

fighting chair, 6, 23, 37
finding fish, 22, 31–33
first-aid kits, 13, 20
fish, deep-sea, types of, 30
fishery biologists, 49
fishfinders, 22

fishing licenses, 17
fishing techniques, 31–35
flatfish, 30

G

gaffs, 20–22, 37
gloves, 25, 43
grouper, 8, 29, 30

H

hauling in and handling fish, 37

I

International Game Fish Association
(IGFA), 29

L

life vests, 13, 18, 23, 39
lines, fishing, 13, 16, 20–22, 23, 25
locations, 29–30
lures, baits, and sinkers, 13, 15, 17, 20, 35
luring fish, 33–35

M

marlin, 30, 38

O

onboard equipment, 18–23
outriggers, 5, 23, 33

P

party boats, 11–13, 15, 17, 18

R

reverse-osmosis water-maker, 22
rod holders, 23
rods and reels, 16, 20

S

safety/precautions, 13, 38–43
seasickness, 40, 41

sobriety, importance of, 40
sun protection, 25, 39

T

tackle/gear, 13, 16–18, 47
tides and currents, 10, 26, 27–28, 33
trolling, 33
tuna, 22, 29, 30, 31, 38

W

water temperature, 28, 29
weather, 23–25, 28
Wildlife and Sport Fish Restoration
    Program, 47

About the Author

Christine Poolos is a writer and editor based in New York City. She has also written on game hunting and record-breaking game harvests.

About the Consultant

Benjamin Cowan has more than twenty years of both freshwater and saltwater angling experience. In addition to being an avid outdoorsman, Cowan is a member of many conservation organizations. He currently resides in west Tennessee.

Photo Credits

Cover, pp. 1, 3, 8, 11, 16, 22, 26, 29, 38, 40, 44, 47 © Fabien Monteil/Shutterstock.com; pp. 4–5, 8, 11, 16, 22, 26, 29, 38, 40, 44, 47 (water) © iStockphoto.com/MichaelJay; pp. 5, 34–35 Ronald C. Modra/Sports Imagery/Getty Images; pp. 9, 12 © The Palm Beach Post/ZUMA Press; p. 14 Boston Globe/Getty Images; pp. 18–19, 39, 41 Orlando Sentinel/McClatchy-Tribune/Getty Images; pp. 20–21 © iStockphoto.com/luxxtek; pp. 24–25 Espen Ørud/Flickr Select/Getty Images; p. 27 © iStockphoto.com/Michael Maywood; pp. 32–33 The Washington Post/Getty Images; pp. 36–37 © Marka/SuperStock; p. 42 © Marianna Day Massey/ZUMA Press; p. 45 © iStockphoto.com/Sam Woolford; p. 48 David Walters/MCT/Landov; p. 50 Jonathan Bird/Peter Arnold/Getty Images; back cover and interior silhouettes (figures) © iStockphoto.com/A-Digit, Hemera/Thinkstock; back cover and interior silhouette (grass) © iStockphoto.com/Makhnach_M; back cover silhouette (hook) iStockphoto.com/Jason Derry.

Designer: Nicole Russo; Photo Researcher: Amy Feinberg